Boost Your Bottom Line

Financial Tips for Consultants

www.consultantsboostyourbottomline.com

Pam Newman, Author

RPPC, Inc.

Realizing Profitable Potential *through* Change

www.rppc.net

Published by Small Business Resources

Missouri

To order this book:

816.304.4398

1.866.206.0824

pam@rppc.net

Published by Small Business Resource

Edited by Cynthia Moran

This publication is designed to provide accurate and authoritative information in regard to the subject matter covered. It is sold with the understanding that the publisher and author are providing information and not specific consultation to your business. The services of a competent professional management accountant should be sought to help you apply this information as needed for your specific situation.

ISBN: 978-0-9764408-1-9

TABLE OF CONTENTS

INTRODUCTION

Looking for a way to be a financially savvy consultant? Then this is the book for you. I trust you know your expertise area well and, therefore, are in the position of looking for ways to utilize the same amount of hours (or less) to increase your profitability. That's what we are going to cover – areas where you can improve your financial aspects. The goal is to not work more hours, but work smarter during the hours you work. Understanding the financial aspects of your business will help you do that. You will also learn an appreciation of what is happening within your business from a numbers' perspective.

The key component to understand is that every decision that is made within the business has a dollars and cents impact. How you set your pricing, what you pay your employees, what type of advertising you do, whether or not you get an office or toll free number, and more. EVERY decision has a dollars and cents impact. What you need to understand is what the impact is for your specific situation.

As an accounting consultant, for more than a decade, I've worked with thousands of different businesses. While everyone has their own story, I find that the story often includes some very similar experiences. While you may be thinking your situation is different, I'd venture to bet that these tips will help you if you are struggling with the business aspects of being a consultant. No matter what your area of specialization, it is still important that you understand the financial aspects of running your business.

Working as a consultant for a large company provides the consultant with the back office assistance that we often don't realize exists until we go out on our own. We know we do the work and we get paid. As an employee we never really focus on the steps in-between. As a consulting business owner, we have to realize that we must think about all those little details, if we truly want to have a well oiled machine that provides us the lifestyle we are looking for. With the areas we will cover in this book, you will feel better prepared to take your business to the next level and enable it to operate as a business should – profitably!

As a consultant, we have very few direct costs in what we provide our clients, as we are sharing our knowledge. That doesn't mean we don't have any costs. Our clients pay us for our knowledge and it is our responsibility to reinvest in ourselves. That obligation takes time and money. Where our costs can get out of control is in our overhead. Spending too much on advertising, automobile expenses (fuel, repairs, leases), office rent, travel, etc. These costs may be legitimate business expenses but what you need to be asking yourself each time you spend a dollar is "what kind of monetary return am I getting on this expenditure?"

One recommendation I make to many small business owners, especially consultants who go to their client's locations or offer services remotely, is, "why pay rent on an office?" I've personally found that I've never had the need to have an office outside my home. If I go to my clients then what benefit would it be for me to have an office? Spending money on things that do not provide a profitable return are not good business decisions. Sometimes our ego can get in the way as we want to appear bigger and better; be careful not to fall in that trap.

My clients don't care that I office from my home. It saves them money in the long run, because I don't have to pass on increased costs. So, in my business model, it is a win-win situation to not have to incur office rent and utility expenses. Besides, I'm a firm believer if you are going to have an office then your clients ought to be coming to your office to receive services. In addition to rent and utilities, you will incur further administrative labor costs because someone has to be there to answer the phone and assist clients, if you have an open door.

If you are going to have an office, make sure that it is contributing to your bottom line. As an accountant, I always stress to my clients that when you spend money it should be for one purpose only – to bring money back to you in multiples. If you spend money in your business for any other reason, you need to seriously reassess why. Are you making choices based on profit or ego? From an accountant's point of view, profit is the only driver for business decisions, as it should be for any consultant. Thus the title "Boost Your Bottom Line," it encapsulates the tips I've shared throughout the book.

Marketing is an important consideration. If clients don't know about you, how can they possibly utilize your services? Marketing is a must for every consultant. The real key is how you choose to spend your marketing dollars and time. Every dollar spent on marketing should bring you revenue. Sometimes it will be a direct relationship, and other times it will be indirect. The key is you need to understand how your marketing dollars impact your bottom line through expenses and revenue. I'll share with you some great cost effective marketing tools, later in this book.

As a business owner, you have a lot of responsibility and flexibility in the way you handle your finances. The key is to know the rules of the financial game so that you stay within those guidelines and don't get yourself into financial trouble. That's why you should have a very good tax accountant on your team to help guide you. You'll see that the goal is not to take away your flexibility, but really to give the power back to you, as the business owner. Of course there are IRS guidelines we need to understand and comply with in our business but there are unlimited ways that you can find your business is a good fit for your particular lifestyle. I suggest you strategically make business decisions instead of running your business in a reactive mode. Every choice you make has an impact, so do you want to know the impact or just have a "wait and see" kind of mentality? I would suggest you take control of your business from a financial perspective and enjoy the benefits that come with it.

The information found in this book should be used for informational and educational purposes only. Consult with your own tax and management accounting specialists for specifics as they relate to your business. In no way am I making specific recommendations to anyone. I'm only sharing my experiences and providing information for you to take into consideration, as you work with your own accounting professional. If you would like specific recommendations, please contact me directly at pam@rppc.net .

DON'T FORGET

Whenever I'm reading, I'm so busy highlighting and making myself notes as to what I want to remember and any new ideas that might arise. Here is a place for you to track those things you don't want to forget:

1.

2.

3.

STRATEGIC BUSINESS MANAGEMENT

There are two ways of running your business – proactive and reactive. Reactive means that you are always "reacting" to the events taking place in your business. While some may not see an issue with this – I do. Reactively running your business decreases your opportunities because you are too busy trying to put out the fires, when your clients call at the last minute, or you are making decisions at the eleventh hour.

Some people view others as being lucky when really luck is there for all of us, if we open ourselves to the possibilities. We must prepare ourselves to be open to take advantage when opportunities present themselves.

Be proactive – stop and think about what you want from your business. Do you have goals? If so, are they written down? How about a business plan? Have you stopped to really think through the various 'what-if's' that you encounter every day? Do you think about things in advance of them happening? A business plan is often thought of as a document that a lender wants to see before they'll consider loaning you money. While that is one purpose of a business plan, the most important reason you would want to have a business plan is for you. You are the one that is going to invest time and money into your business. Don't you want to have a well thought out plan as to where you want your business to go? What you hope to achieve with this business? How you want to accomplish your mission and make money?

No matter how long you have been in business, you can benefit from having a business plan. Some of the key components of a business plan are:

1. Statement of purpose - What is the business going to do? Ensure you are answering: Who, What, Why, When, and Where.
2. Core Parts:
    i. The Business
        1. Description of business
        2. Competition
        3. Marketing
        4. Operating procedures

5. Financial data
6. Business insurance
7. Personnel

ii. Financial Data

1. Balance sheet
2. Capital equipment and supply list
3. Loan applications
4. Breakeven analysis
5. Pro-forma income projections (profit & loss statements)
    a. Three-year summary
    b. Detail by month for the first year.
6. Detail by quarters for the second and third years.
    a. Assumptions upon which projections were based.
7. Pro-forma cash flow
    a. Detail your inflow and outflows.

iii. Supporting Documents - Needed if you are looking for financing.

1. Tax returns of principals
2. Personal Financial Statements
    a. Income Statement (Revenues and Expenses)
    b. Balance Sheet (Assets/Liabilities/Equity).

This book is not designed to teach you how to create a business plan. There are many great resources already on the market that can assist you with that. In addition, you can contact your local Small Business Development Center for personal guidance in the creation of your business plan. I just want you to realize that it is important to have one that you use as part of your overall strategic management process in guiding your company down the road of growth and profitability.

If you are too busy to be strategic in running your business then you will be running without a focus. Decide if you want to spend more time working in your business or on your business. It is a combination of both areas that most consultants find successful.

DON'T FORGET

1.

2.

3.

OVERHEAD

Overhead is an accumulation of all those "other" expenses you incur in your business that are not direct material or labor costs. They can be costs that are legitimate business expenses, but the question you need to be asking yourself is "how does this expenditure help me generate revenue?" If you can't answer that question, then you need to reconsider whether or not you should have the expense.

Overhead can eat up your profitability and make you wonder if all the work you do is really worth it. Ever feel like you are working 24/7 and not getting anywhere? Then it is time to reassess why. As a consultant, often times our direct costs of material and labor are nominal. So the place where our money must be leaking away is in the overhead.

Look at how much you are spending on these areas:

- Rent
- Utilities
- Insurance
- Administrative Staff
- Telephone/Internet
- Office Supplies
- Professional Services
- Continuing Education

The number one area I see most new consultants spend money on unnecessarily is rental of an office when there is no "business" need to do so. Every expense that you incur as a consultant should have an impact on your revenue generating capabilities. If an office does not help you generate revenue then why do you have it? Running your business from your home is a great cost effective measure, especially in the beginning. As your business grows, then assess the “need” to have an office. Most find that there is really never a “need” to have an outside office, because they are never there anyway.

It’s time for you to get a clear understanding of where your dollars are going. Take the dollars that you are spending in each of these overhead areas and divide it by the amount of income you earn in that same time period. Time period analysis is normally by the month, quarter, or year. By dividing the dollar amount of a specific expense by the total revenue, it will provide you with a percentage of your expenses compared to your income. In other words, you have 100% of revenue when you charge your clients for your services. Now what do you do with that revenue? You spend it on direct costs and overhead. So if your ratio of advertising is 10%, then that means that you spend 10 cents out of every dollar you generate on advertising.

DON'T FORGET

1.

2.

3.

FINANCIAL STATEMENTS

If you want to be a profitable consultant, it is imperative that you have a basic understanding of the financial aspect of running your business. Don't worry! If this isn't your area of expertise, then work with an accountant. People pay for your expertise. It is not uncommon to think you'll need to do the same! There is no reason you would not want to understand the financial components of your business except that you are avoiding the obvious. So step up to the challenge and learn the basics of running your business from a financial perspective. You should have four main financial reports that you need to know:

1. Profit & Loss Statement
2. Balance Sheet
3. Cash Flow Statement
4. Accounts Receivable Aging

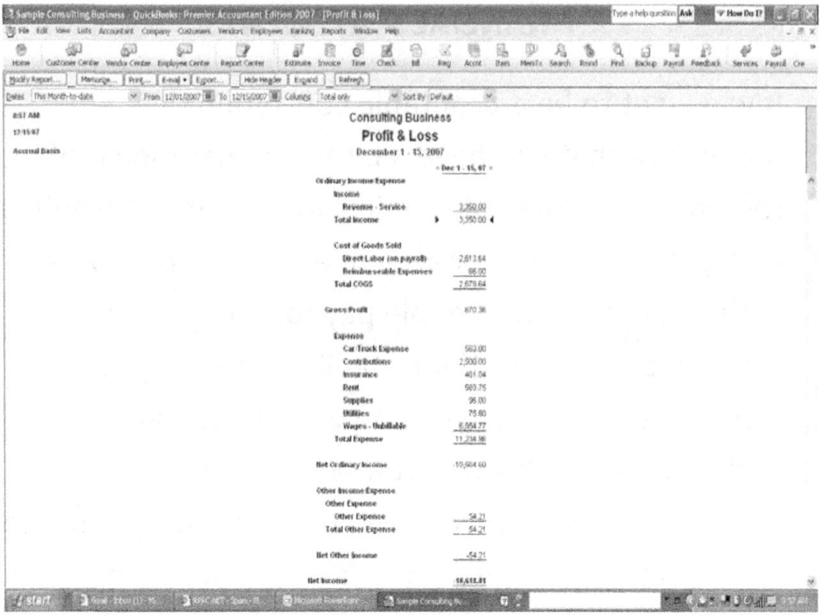

Figure 1: Profit & Loss Statement

The Profit & Loss Statement provides an accounting of the income and expenses that you have incurred for any given time period you have selected. Monitoring this on a monthly basis enables you to keep tabs on where your money is coming from and going to. Ignoring what is happening doesn't change things. It just puts you in a position of ignorance because you have no clue what's really happening.

The Profit & Loss Statement provides an overview for a period of time (usually monthly, quarterly or yearly) of the income and expenses for the business. Income represents the value of your products and services. Cost of Goods Sold (aka Cost of Services Provided) is the direct costs for labor and materials. Direct costs mean that they are directly related to the product or service you provide. Expenses are the overhead expenses that your business incurs such as rent, taxes, administrative assistance, marketing, office supplies, professional fees, continuing education, etc.

The Profit and Loss Statement should also be viewed at the project level. It is important that as a consultant you understand your profitability for each client (or project) you work on.

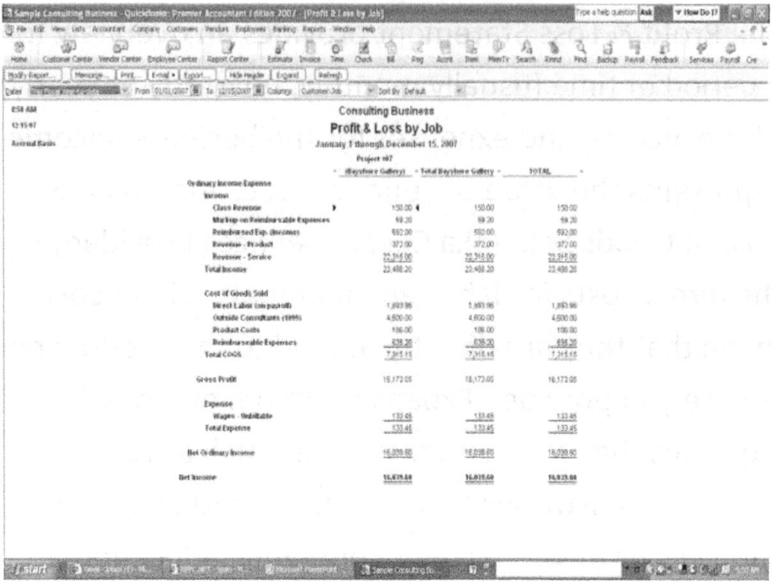

Figure 2: Profit & Loss Statement by Job

When you are monitoring the profitability within your company, it should include the detailed level by each project you work on.

Utilizing a system like QuickBooks® to track your income and expenses will assist you. You can find out more information at www.rppc.net or www.quickbooks.com. When you have a project, your costs associated with that project should be documented so that, at the end of the project, you can assess whether it was a good project for you.

In QuickBooks® this would be done by setting up customers and jobs in your Customer: Job List. Then you would attach a customer and job reference to each cost you incur for a job. It's a simple bookkeeping tracking option and the reporting that you will then get is very valuable.

If you made $1000 but spent $1200, then it will be obvious to you that it wasn't a good fit. That information then enables you to go back and assess what went wrong. Was there some kind of rework that took place that escalated the costs higher than anticipated? Was it a new type of project for you causing the learning curve to be a little longer then it will be for future projects? Or do you simply need to have a better handle on which projects you select to participate in? This analysis is simple, if you have reliable information easily available. Using systems such as QuickBooks® enables you to have that – so there are no more excuses!

There are two main ways that we bill for our services – by the hour and lump sum by the project. You will hear many different opinions on which are best. From my perspective, when you bill by the project, and you are efficient, you have an increased opportunity for higher profitability. When you bill by the hour, your profitability by hour is predetermined, but you ensure you are compensated for the hours you put in. Which is right or wrong? I believe neither – you have to be the one to find the best fit for your offerings, your business model and your clients.

In the world of accounting, I find that most businesses are like opening a can of worms. They believe their issues are small and maybe they would even appear that way to me. But more likely than not, when I start digging in I find out that there are many more issues behind the scenes that need to be addressed. If I committed to a fixed contract then I would be assuming the risk. I find it more of a fit with the majority of my clients to do it on an hourly investment basis.

As I uncover issues, I share them with my clients and discuss the pros and cons of addressing whatever the issue may be. The clients then know, based upon my hourly rate, what their fees will be. This enables me to put the risk on the client's plate, as it is their business and I'm the consultant there to help them. I always want to approach it as a win-win solution, not a win-lose.

Though I know many of my competitors prefer to do it as a fixed contract arrangement, as they feel they have more opportunity for profit. Again, I don't believe either way is a fit for all businesses, so you need to make the call that best fits your business model. Work with your professional management accountant to help assess pros/cons of both options for your business model. If you want to brainstorm with me, feel free to contact me at pam@rppc.net .

For those who allow their clients to pay on account, it is important that you manage your accounts receivable with an AR Aging Report.

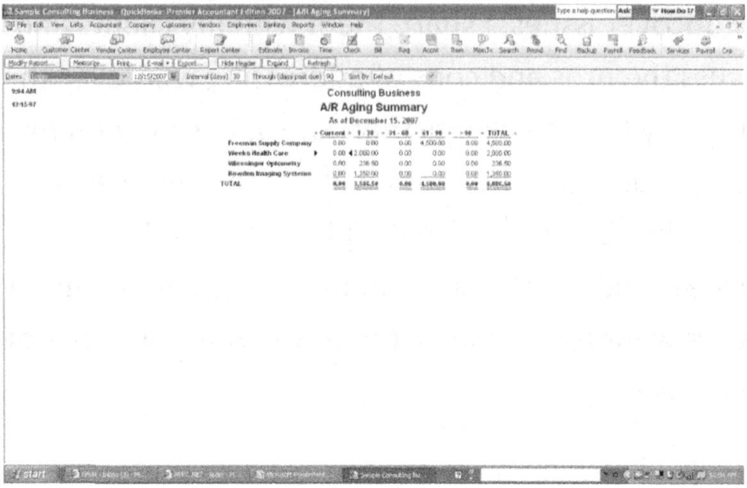

Figure 3: Accounts Receivable Aging Summary

The longer it takes your clients to pay, the less likely you are to collect. This type of report provides you with the information to see which clients owe you money and how past due they are.

Just remember that when you spend time on administrative activities, such as collections, you are not doing billable work that generates revenue. Minimize non-value added activities such as collecting past due accounts. This is a prime example of how a little proactive work, getting your contracts in place and payment ahead of time, will alleviate the need for follow-up collection activities.

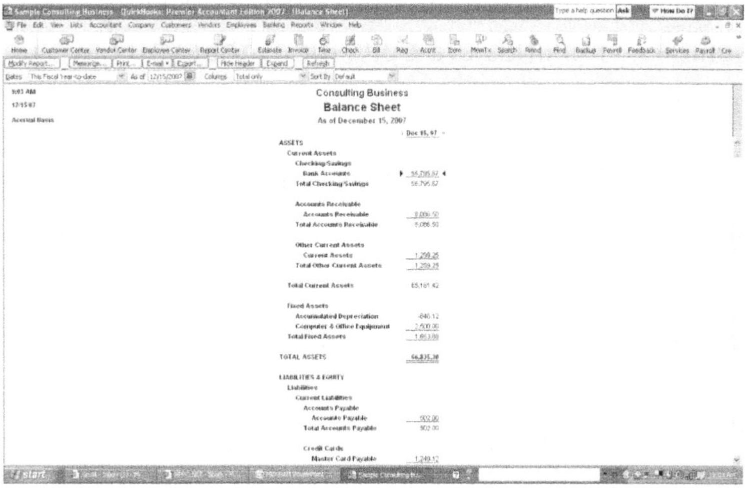

Figure 4: Balance Sheet

The above picture shows the beginning of the Balance Sheet with an outline of the various assets and liabilities that this sample company has. You will notice that assets include bank accounts, accounts receivable, and any kind of fixed assets one may have such as computers, desks, equipment, vehicles, etc.

The following picture is the second half of the Balance Sheet which outlines the liabilities that may include amounts owed to vendors for advertising, utilities, and any other kind of day-to-day operating bills. Credit cards and loans are also considered liabilities. Liabilities are obligations that you have to pay someone else.

When you enter a bill in QuickBooks® for an expense such as advertising, you will classify it as an expense so it populates on your Profit & Loss Statement. The fact that you have not yet paid the bill will also result in a liability until you pay it. Equity is the resulting net of Assets-Liabilities to show the amount of ownership you have in the business.

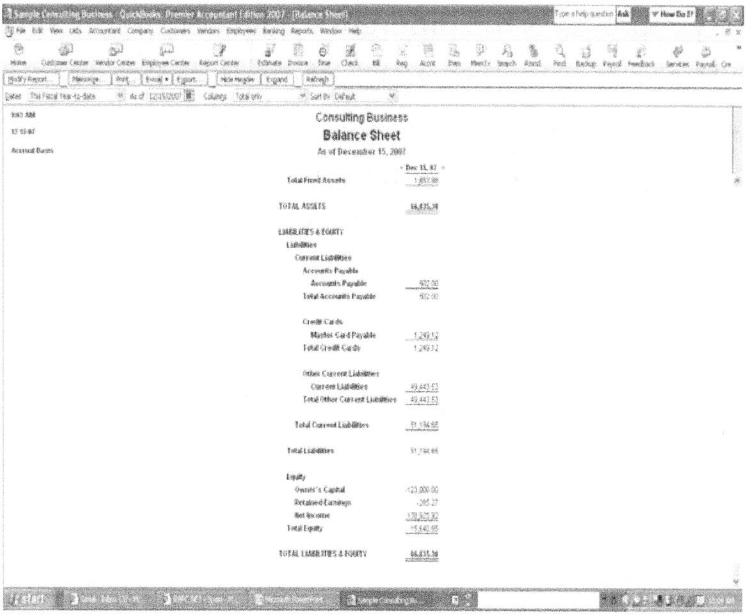

Figure 5: Balance Sheet Continued

In Summary, the Balance Sheet provides an overview of the assets, liabilities, and equity of the business. Assets represent what you own such as office equipment, cash, and accounts receivable. Liabilities consist of what you owe to someone else such as banks, lenders and credit card companies. Equity is the difference between what you own and what you owe. It includes any cash or other items you contribute or take from the business personally.

Equity represents the difference between assets and liabilities and is the net worth of our business. For example, if your assets are $100 and your liabilities are $40, then your equity is $60.

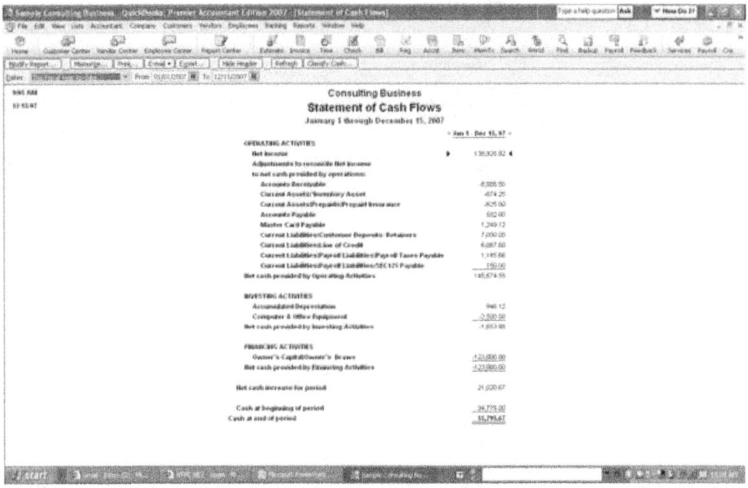

Figure 6: Statement of Cash Flows

Cash Flow is different than profitability so it is important to understand what type of loan and credit card payments you are making out of your profitability. In addition, it is important that you have a plan on how you are compensating yourself. Is it through payroll expense and/or draws? Traditionally, as business owners, we do a combination of both payroll expense and equity draws, as each has different tax aspects. Cash Flow Statements provide us an understanding of where our cash is coming from and going to. So it is important that you understand that cash is different than profit. You can be profitable and have a negative cash flow. This happens when your liability payments are greater than your profit.

QuickBooks® is a registered trademark of Intuit and is used as a reference only.

DON'T FORGET

1.

2.

3.

ESTABLISHING A PRICING MODEL

It is critical as a consultant to understand the value that you bring to the table. While you may have some products to sell, the majority of what you provide is intangible. It is up to you to prove to your clientele that you are worth the money. There are seven key considerations when establishing your prices:

1. What is your unique offering? What makes you different then your competitors? If you are not different, then they will not see the value in working with you over anyone else. You do not want them to be price sensitive to the point that they are looking for the lowest dollar consultant. Who wants to be in that position? I don't, and I discourage you from being, either. You want them to see that you can add value to their business, based upon your unique experiences and knowledge, and that is why they would be willing to spend their hard earned dollars working with you. That is what

enables you to charge and justify the prices that you do.

2. What pains do your clients have that you help eliminate? Your clients have some need for wanting to work with you. So what are you going to do to improve their world? You are the one that will lead them through that discovery phase of identifying their pains and providing solutions.

3. What are the benefits your clients receive by working with you? Really – when it all boils down, most clients want their benefits to be around two main areas: time and money. You need to be able to clearly express the desired benefits that your clients receive from working with you.

4. Understanding your costs – direct and indirect. Don't only think about your day-to- day costs, but what about the investment that you need to make in yourself professionally to keep on top of your game? You should be able to use a

computerized accounting system, such as QuickBooks® to track your expenses (direct and indirect) so that you have a clear understanding of what it takes to operate your business. If you don't know your costs, how can you possibly have any idea if you are making a profit?

5. Market Analysis. While you need to be aware of what is happening in your market and understand the pros and cons of your competitors, this is only one aspect of your pricing model. Remember marketing class and SWOT (Strengths, Weaknesses, Opportunities and Threats) Analysis? Here you need to be assessing what your internal strengths and weaknesses are and the threats and opportunities that you are surrounded with.

6. Your goals – what are your goals? You need to have a clear understanding of the bull's-eye you are aiming for, before you throw your first dart! This is where your business plan comes in

handy – it helps you to identify your goals and what you want out of your business.

7. Sanity check. You must understand the reality of your world and do a sanity check to ensure your pricing model is viable. If it sounds too good to be true, it probably is. If you aren't going to make any money – find a different career and don't waste your time on being a consultant.

Utilizing these seven areas to guide you in developing your pricing model will help you to have a strategic plan of how you are going to operate your business profitably. Your pricing model is a key component to your success because, obviously, if you aren't charging enough for your services, there won't be any revenue for sustained existence.

You may also find that as your business evolves your pricing model will change. The key is to understand how you can make your services profitable for you and value-added for your clients. As your goals for your business change and your client's needs change, these will impact your business pricing model. It is not a static aspect of your business. Your pricing model constantly needs to be reassessed, as your internal and external business environment changes.

DON'T FORGET

1.

2.

3.

CONTRACT PROCESSES

It is no longer the age of a hand shake. While we always want to give our clients the benefit of the doubt, misunderstandings do occur. Therefore, it requires you to have a contract in place to ensure both parties are clear on what they are providing and receiving. Do not leave relationships to chance. Approach a contract as a way of ensuring that the client understands how the process will work. The fact is you are providing a contract as much for their benefit as yours; it will be for the benefit of all parties.

The number one thing you should do is have a written contract that your attorney has reviewed. It doesn't have to be long. I try to keep mine to one page. Short, sweet, and to the point, so that there is less room for error in interpretation. You don't want to make it a hassle for them to work with you.

There are a few things I've implemented that I have found to be very successful. The first is the practice of having a credit card on file at the beginning of the relationship. Your time is not well spent on doing collections; avoid those hassles up front. Here's how I've implemented it within my company:

1. First of all, no appointment is scheduled without having a client agreement and credit card on file. Mine is one page and we email or fax it to them and follow-up to ensure we receive the signed copy back within 48 hours.

2. Any client who is unwilling to share their credit card is not serious about working with you. Therefore, there is no reason for you to waste your time. Your time is valuable and if you set aside your time specifically to work with them, then you should be compensated. If they have nothing to lose, they do not value your time.

3. Have a cancellation policy outlined. Again, we cannot recapture our time if it expires and the client chooses not to meet with us, particularly at the last moment. So, I've implemented a 48-

hour cancellation policy. Our office calls them 48 hours in advance of the scheduled appointment to remind the client of the upcoming meeting. This provides them a friendly reminder and an opportunity to reschedule, should they have a conflict with their schedule. Cancelling after that time requires them to pay for the scheduled consultation time.

My normal consultation is held in 3 hour increments. Clients that miss scheduled meetings would be billed for that full amount. I rarely schedule an all day consultation for one client because I find it is more productive to do smaller time frames (3 hours). This also minimizes my schedule opening up a full day, at the last moment, that cannot be rebooked with another client.

In addition, I don't want other clients having to wait unnecessarily for a future date when I could have seen them earlier. My schedule normally books about 2 to 3 weeks in advance for personal on-sites, so I try to use those client hours wisely. Training and speaking engagements are scheduled months in advance.

I always have plenty of work to do in the office, though I know that I have a goal of a certain number of onsite billable hours per week with clients. This will be discussed further in the BREAKEVEN POINT section.

4. Deposits are a must for any speaking engagements. This day will be reserved for the event and it is customary that a deposit is paid to reserve the date. The deposit should always be nonrefundable, as you are potentially turning away other paid opportunities that you won't be able recapture if the date were to reopen at a later time. Usually one-third to one-half is customary with the remainder paid on the day of the speaking event.

5. Do not carry receivables. All client work should be paid in advance, or on the day of the service. Spending time handling receivables is not a value added process. Having a credit card on file makes this the most simple of all processes, as you can process their credit card when you return to the office and email them a receipt. No messy paperwork or follow-up collections needed. Everything is clean and quick.

6. I utilize credit card processing within my computerized bookkeeping system. No extra software or hardware is needed and everything is handled seamlessly through my accounting system. It can't get any easier than that. Make it simple as you have many other areas that need your time!

DON'T FORGET

1.

2.

3.

COMPUTERIZED BOOKKEEPING SYSTEM

Welcome to the new era – it is an era that functions on computers. Why would you not have a computerized system? I can't think of any reason you should not. Spreadsheets are not enough. They provide no easy way to produce financial statements. My guess is that you aren't in business to be a bookkeeper, but you are in business to make money and provide a service.

Based on my years of experience as an accounting consultant, I've never encountered a business owner (other than those who were opening an accounting/bookkeeping business) that looked forward to doing the book work in their business. It is the number one thing that entrepreneurs, in general, do not like about being a business owner. Regardless of your like or dislike, it is a necessary part of running a business. Let's address how you can make your bookkeeping easier!

Start with bookkeeping software that is easy to get support for. That way, as you are learning the software, you will have someone to help you. I specialize in QuickBooks® because it has a proven track record; it's easy to find someone local to assist you and it is very cost-effective. Rarely is it necessary for a consultant to order any kind of special bookkeeping software. There are always exceptions, but most of the time cost-effective software off the shelf will provide you with the tools that you need. The other option is you can outsource it to someone who can provide the bookkeeping services. Just ensure they are using a computerized system.

Remember when you look to outsource that you are still ultimately responsible for good books. I find that sometimes, when consultants are devaluing the information they can get in their financials, they are not willing to pay for quality assistance. It amazes me that, as consultants, we bill for our time and we want our clients to appreciate the value. Yet, when we look for professional services, we often do not follow our own advice. You get what you pay for is often what I find. Hire someone who knows what they are doing and can help you understand your financials, and incorporate that into the overall business management strategy you have for your company.

The whole goal of bookkeeping is that you want to be able to easily track your income and your expenses. To be able to compile that information in a useful format requires the function of being able to produce financial statements such as:

1. Profit & Loss Statement
2. Profit & Loss by Project
3. Balance Sheet
4. Cash Flow
5. Accounts Receivable Aging

Examples of these can be found earlier in this book – see area on Financial Statements. The key is that it has to be computerized so that it can track the day-to-day activities and provide you financial statements when needed.

Included in the offerings of the software should also be the ability to:

1. General checkbook functionality
2. Invoicing
3. Project Costing
4. Estimating (i.e. proposals)
5. Tracking Bills
6. Reports

Some software will have more or fewer features, but I consider these the six necessary aspects any business owner should be able to have in their system. Purchasing a more complex system should be assessed with an open minded. If you will not be using the features then you are wasting your money and making it more difficult to learn.

Don't go with personal bookkeeping software, as it will not offer you the invoicing and reporting features that you will need as a business owner. Visit with others in your profession for industry specific recommendations, as well as your accountant for general software recommendations. As a consultant, I recommend to my clients an "off the shelf" product such as QuickBooks®, as it is very cost competitive and meets most any need I've found a consultant to have (other than a calendar or scheduling component, but this can be fulfilled using Outlook® or a similar product).

DON'T FORGET

1.

2.

3.

PROJECT COSTING

Project costing is concept that is often overlooked in the consulting arena. In general, people automatically think of the construction industry as being project focused. In reality there are literally thousands of professions that are project based, including the consulting arena. Project costing is an important part of running a business when there are individual projects or jobs that are happening. Why? By breaking down the profitability on a per-project basis you are better able to assess which projects are good choices and which are not. That is the key.

There will come a time when you are so busy that you will be turning away jobs or running yourself into your grave. Stop before you start that behavior. Project costing provides you the tools to understand how to assess which jobs meet your profitability goals and which do not. That way, as you move forward, you will be able to say “yes” to the projects that are profitable and “no” to those that are not (or at least those that are less profitable).

Project costing, at its simplest level, is taking each dollar of revenue and expense, and attaching it to a project (if applicable). Using a program such as QuickBooks® will allow you to see the revenues and costs associated with each project. Overhead expenses such as advertising, rent, administrative labor, and other general business expenses are not directly tied to the projects. You will be able to allocate a portion of your overhead to each project to get the full project costs. Allocation, in its simplest format, is taking your total overhead and dividing it out over your projects. For example, if you had $1000 of overhead a month (rent, utilities, advertising, administrative labor, etc) and you bill out 100 hours of time then you would want to allocate an additional $10 of overhead cost to each hour spent on a project. There are a variety of ways to allocate overhead and you can visit with your business management accountant to discuss the specifics that will be easiest and most accurate for you to track.

If you don't know how much you are making on each consulting project, then how are you able to assess whether or not you are going to reach your financial goals for your business? The checkbook balance only tells you how much cash you have; it doesn't tell you your profitability. Breaking profitability analysis down to each project allows you to then focus your time and resources on those projects that will bring you the greatest financial return. Having lots of clients doesn't make us profitable. We want to be selective so that we are spending our limited amount of time with those clients that we can add the most value to and receive the most financial rewards from. That is a true win-win situation.

DON'T FORGET

1.

2.

3.

BREAKEVEN POINT

Your breakeven point is the point at which your income equals your expenses. At your breakeven point there is no profit and there is no loss. You must understand what your breakeven point is before you can realize a profit.

As a consultant, we'll focus on the fact that it is mainly services you are providing, to keep it simple for this equation. I do realize that some of you will sell products and that is an area where you can work in more detail with me or your individual accountant. When I use the term "units" it can be hours or number of products, depending on your specific situation.

As a consultant, we only have so many hours that we can provide services. When we are setting financial goals we need to take into account the number of hours we will bill out and the rate at which we will bill our hours. Revenue equals quantity multiplied by the rate. If you bill out 20 hours a month at a rate of $100 then your revenue for the month will be $2,000.

You must be aware that this calculation does not tell you if you are covering your expenses or being profitable. So how do you know that? Determine first what your breakeven is and then the hours above and beyond that will bring your profitability.

Let's assume these are your monthly costs:

Administrative Labor	$ 800
Insurance	$ 300
Office Supplies	$ 100
Networking/Marketing	$ 100
Travel	$ 400
Professional Education	$ 300
Total Expenses	$2,000

I realize there are many more types of expenses you might have, but let's keep it simple for demonstration purposes! If your monthly expenses are $2000 then that is your breakeven point. Once you reach $2000 of revenue, anything beyond that provides you profit. This simple model assumes the $2000 of cost is incurred each month regardless of how much revenue you generate and, therefore, are considered "fixed" costs. Fixed costs do not fluctuate based upon activity.

In this simple example, once you have billed 20 hours at $100 then you have reached your breakeven point. Each hour over 20 for the month will provide profit to your bottom line, on your Profit & Loss Statement. So if you have 30 hours of billable time in the month, your profit would be 10 hours at $100 for a profit of $1000.

Let's look at a little more complex model, for those who have variable costs as well. If you have project costs that are directly related to your projects then those are called "variable" costs, because they vary with activity. So with any additional variable costs, your breakeven will change. As consultants, if we provide strictly a service, there are usually no direct costs involved, if it is for local clients. When we travel, or provide products for our clients, then there becomes a direct cost associated with our offerings.

If your business model includes products or travel, where you do incur extra costs with the delivery of products or services for your clients, then this will be your breakeven model:

Sales

Less Direct (Variable) Costs

= Contribution Margin

Contribution margin is how much out of each dollar of revenue you have to "contribute" towards your fixed costs, once you have covered your direct (variable) costs.

You will then take your Fixed Costs and divide it by the gross profit margin to determine how many billable hours you must have to breakeven.

To calculate your breakeven point using this model, let's assume your fixed costs are still $2,000 but that your variable cost with each hour of service you provide is $20.

Your contribution margin on each hour of service is:

$100 (Revenue)

Less $20 (Direct Cost)

Equals Contribution Margin of $80 per hour

Using this model to breakeven then you would have to divide your $2000 of fixed costs by the $80/hour contribution margin. This will equate to 25 hours of billable time to breakeven.

Revenue 25 @ $100	$2,500
Direct Costs 25 @ $20	($ 500)
Gross Profit	$2,000
Indirect Costs	($2,000)
Profit/Loss	$ 0

Information for the breakeven calculation can be found on your Profit & Loss Statement. If you need help doing this calculation, contact your accountant or me, at pam@rppc.net and I will be happy to help you!

Why is it important to know your breakeven important? Ask the millions of consultants who work a crazy amount of hours but never feel like they are making ends meet. ***Being busy doesn't equate to being profitable.*** If you don't know how many hours you need to bill to breakeven then how will you ever know how many you need to achieve your profitability goals? Know your breakeven and you'll be on your way to boosting your bottom line.

DON'T FORGET

1.

2.

3.

YOUR CALCULATION

Revenue:

Direct Costs:

Contribution Margin:

Breakeven Calculation:

UNDERSTANDING YOUR COSTS

Understanding costs can be a black hole for most consultants. They don't have a clear grasp of what their full costs are. When assessing your costs, you need to consider your direct project costs, your overhead, and the ongoing education and growth of your business. You aren't in business (I assume) to breakeven or just barely get by. If that's the model you are going with, you will experience burnout quite rapidly.

It is vital to remember that our clients are relying on us to be well versed in our area of specialty; not only historically but recent trends, as well. We have to nourish our minds to keep on top where our clients will want to pay us for our knowledge and experiences. It is our duty to make certain we deliver and exceed their expectations. Make sure to include those expectations for yourself as well when you are setting your prices.

In my experience, consultants tend to undercharge for their services, because they don't understand how all the costs play into the profitability equation. The fact that there are minimal to no direct costs misleads consultants to believe that their billable rate is profit. To reiterate points made earlier in the book, that is not the case. From the billable revenue, you need to subtract out both direct and indirect costs to achieve profitability.

One of the most important aspects that you need to take into consideration, when looking at your costs, is the investment you make in yourself. You are selling your knowledge. Acquiring that knowledge has cost associated with it – both actual costs and the value of your time. When you take a week off to go to a conference, you have lost opportunity cost because you can't be billing out your hours for the week. In addition, you are going to incur costs for travel, conference registration fees, meals, etc. Those types of costs have to be accounted for during the times you are billing your clients for services provided.

Sure your clients might be able to acquire similar knowledge, but do they have the time? When I hire a professional, it's not necessarily because I CAN'T figure out the knowledge on my own. It simply is a time issue. Do I have the time to acquire the knowledge and does that make sense for me to spend my time acquiring the knowledge? For example, when my clients need help with their information technology systems I don't help them. I find resources to fulfill their needs who are already an expert in that field, versus me trying to be all things to all people. Why would I, or my clients, pay them? The reason is their years of experience and knowledge enables them to provide a solution immediately. This, in turn, allows us to move on to the areas that enable my client to generate revenue more immediately, versus acquiring knowledge outside of our area of specialty.

As a consultant, one of the best things we can do is surround ourselves with other professionals who compliment our knowledge. It enables us to have a greater pool of resources and solve our client's issues more efficiently and effectively. That is the key! That is the same reason people pay you – so that you can solve their needs efficiently and effectively! Know your worth and your costs, and charge accordingly. It is not bad to make a profit. You must realize that – some people have an issue with making profit and therefore only hold themselves back. If you provide a good value to your clients, then you deserve to have a fair profit.

DON'T FORGET

1.

2.

3.

QUESTIONS I WANT TO ASK MY ACCOUNTANT

1.

2.

3.

UNIQUE SELLING PROPOSITION

If you can't think of anything that makes you different from everybody else, then neither will your clients. Is that truly what you want to be? Not me – I want to make a memorable impression. This is not the time to be like everyone else and try to fit in with the crowd.

Differentiation is the key to success. This is what will enable you to set your fees higher and become an expert.

People want to do business with others they feel are experts and knowledgeable. Ask yourself what kind of presentation you provide to others. Are you the expert in your field? It is often joked about in my area that people know me related to what I provide – even if they don't know my name. All they have to do is ask around and word of mouth will lead them to me. This is the position you want to be in. Differentiation leads you down the path of greatness.

Creating more than just your consulting service is the key for growth. As a consultant, you only have so many hours that you can bill out. You need to ask yourself how can you earn more and be more. It's by thinking of yourself as an "infopreneur" – you provide information to your clients and that's not just by meeting with them. How can you sell your information in other ways? Consider offering books, speaking services, teleseminars, tapes, videos, group consulting, and more.

These areas provide great marketing tools as well as revenue generating tools. Enjoy the double benefit you will receive. Consensus among consultants is that if you truly want to be at the top of the consulting pyramid, you will have to be a resource provider with a larger scale of offerings other than one-on-one consulting. Every one of us has a goal for ourselves. If your goal is to be a profitable "infopreneur", then you must not limit your thinking. We can be our own worst enemy by having self limiting thoughts. That limits our success monetarily and intrinsically. ***Believe in yourself.***

Ask yourself “why not?” every day. Think about what you could be doing that you are not. Don’t say, because you haven’t ever done it before…Just say “why not” and do it!

DON'T FORGET

1.

2.

3.

CREATIVE MARKETING

There are ways to market your business. One often underutilized option is taking advantage of creative marketing opportunities. There a lot of paid marketing aspects you can consider. While marketing is always an important part of running a business, it should contain a mixture of options. Some that I find are most often overlooked are the following options.

Three areas to consider implementing in your mix include:

1. Articles

2. Speaking

3. Books

There are always publications looking for articles. Submit articles to local newspapers, industry specific newspapers, newsletters and anyone else that would afford you a forum for readers interested in what you have to say. Most of the time these will be unpaid opportunities but the benefits can be great. I find that this type of marketing far exceeds any kind of paid advertising I might be able to implement within my business. Writing gives you a certain status of expert within your field. You never know who will see your article and be interested in working with you. Don't shy away if you are not directly compensated for writing, look at it as an investment in building your reputation.

I have had opportunities come from writing to include radio spokesperson, writing for www.entrepreneur.com and various other publications, speaking for national trade shows and conventions. Was it worth my time? DEFINITELY! I see it as a way of building my portfolio and extending my reach in the business community.

Speaking is another untapped opportunity for most consultants. There are always a number of organizations looking for speakers at their luncheons, trade shows, networking events, and any other reason they can come up with to have a gathering of people. This is an opportunity that you should take advantage of; there will be multiple benefits. First is that the more you speak to people, the better communicator you become. Who can't use that benefit? We all need to be good communicators, whether it is in a one-on-one environment or you are speaking in front of a group. Secondly, speaking allows people to get to know you. When people know and like you, they are more likely to do business with you. So stop just being a "name" and actually let people see the real you in personal situations where you are presenting. Third, speaking is a great marketing opportunity. Instead of paying for advertising, you are getting the opportunity to market yourself for free. Sometimes you can even get paid for it. Paid for marketing yourself? Wow – why wouldn't you want to do that? But be cautious.

When I say, "get paid for marketing yourself," I want you to understand that there are guidelines on how to do that so that it doesn't come across as a sales pitch. Sales pitches are not good in this environment, as it will turn people off. Make certain you understand that by marketing yourself I mean you will be sharing your knowledge and that is what will make people want to work with you. It is a soft marketing – when you share your knowledge with people and they see the benefits of what you can do for them. They will want to do business with you. It's a fine line that you must learn how to straddle.

The keys to having an effective speaking engagement are:

1. Know your audience.
2. Educate your audience.
3. Be enthusiastic.
4. Be knowledgeable.
5. Be unique.

Know your audience – when you are giving a presentation, you need to tailor it to the audience members. Most any company or organization will have a website, so make sure you visit it and learn all you can. If it is an organization, they will often have a list of members that will allow you to get an even deeper understanding of the organization and its membership. Arrive early to your presentation, so that you can mingle. Audience members want to be able to relate to you so be prepared to interact prior to your presentation.

Educate your audience – while some speakers have the luxury of being only expected to entertain, your audience will respond better when you teach them something. It is a rare event that it will be strictly entertainment your audience is looking for; unless you are a comedian. Assuming that you are not a comedian, your audience is looking to you for information; they want you to educate them. Teach them something they don't know, but make sure you give them easy-to-implement tips. Audiences want to be able to take back the information and implement your ideas easily.

We've all been to seminars that we enjoyed, but forgot the information as soon as we left. The key to being an effective presenter is to motivate our audience to action, by giving them good information. Don't forget to let them know that, if they need help implementing those tips, you are available. If they see you as an expert and see how the information you have shared could impact their bottom line, then they will be interested!

Be enthusiastic – don't present in a monotone way. How boring will that be? Be enthusiastic about your topic. If you can't be enthusiastic, then you need to ask yourself why you are the presenter. Your audience can't be expected to enjoy something you don't enjoy. Find a topic you love and enthusiasm will be natural. Just make sure that you are not overly chaotic in your enthusiasm though. Channel your enthusiasm and let it flow through your presentation so that it is motivating and intriguing to your clients.

Be knowledgeable – You need to be a lifelong learner in your field of choice. If you believe you have arrived to a position where there is no more for you to learn, then you have become stale. You need to be up-to-date with the latest happenings. I always ask people how they stay current in their field of choice. When they can't easily give me an answer then I question what I can really learn from them. I never believe that I have "arrived" where I know it all and that I can stop learning. There is always something for me to learn. That is what my clients pay me for and I owe it to them to deliver. When I am speaking in front of a group, I never claim to know it all. I am there to share my knowledge and my experiences.

I personally don't like it when people throw around the term of "expert" loosely. Some people would assume that means them (or I) know it all. Never would I make such a claim. Do I know a lot about my field of choice? Sure I do. I am also keenly aware that there is always something for me to learn and there will always be experiences that I've not personally experienced. I get exposed to more situations then just my personal ones because of the interactions that I have with my clients. I learn through their experiences and this affords me a large pool to drawn upon, but there is always opportunity for me to learn more. **Never stop learning.** Let your audience see that you are knowledgeable and that you are always eager to learn more so that you can share with them!

Be unique – Don't be like everyone else. There are moments in your life when you may want to blend in with the crowd. However, that should not be your goal in business. If you are like everyone else then you are a commodity. Therefore, if I am your potential client, why would I choose to work with you over your competitors? Being like everyone else leaves you little to market yourself on, outside of price. Price wars are not a good business model. Who wants to be the low price offering in their area of specialty? Not me. Pricing provides little opportunity for long-term client relationships. If they have "shopped" you for price, you need to be aware that there will always be someone willing to undercut your price.

Another way to differentiate yourself is by writing. Writing books can be intimidating for some. Some people feel that they don't have enough information to share to write a book. You don't have to write a novel. Keep it short and sweet is a great principle to follow; especially when you are starting out. People are so busy today that they don't take much time to read. Keep your thoughts simple and easy to follow. I always say they should be able to read my books in one sitting within a couple of hours.

Don't know what to write about? What is your area of expertise? That is what you should write about. If you work with clients every day to help them then just take that same knowledge and put it down on paper. There are many ways to do that and ample software tools that can help you if you are not a good typist. There are tools available that enable you to simply speak and it types the information for you. You can also use call-in services that allow you to basically speak into a phone, or tape recorder, and someone will transcribe the information for you.

Another great way to get started with a book is to take some of your articles and expand upon them. If you have an article that is “10 Tips for ....” you have an outline for your book. Just take those tips and expand on them, with three or four major points under each tip. Give a few examples and you have a book. It might only be 100 pages, but that is perfect for a short book that you can use as lead generator and revenue producer for your business.

Don’t worry about how you are going to find someone to publish your book. Self publishing is the way to go. If the opportunity later arises that a well known publisher wants to discuss business with you, then you can cross that bridge when you get to it. Self publishing is a relatively simple process that can be expanded upon as your business model. So what better way to make yourself unique in your industry then to publish a book?

DON'T FORGET

1.

2.

3.

INDUSTRY INFORMATION

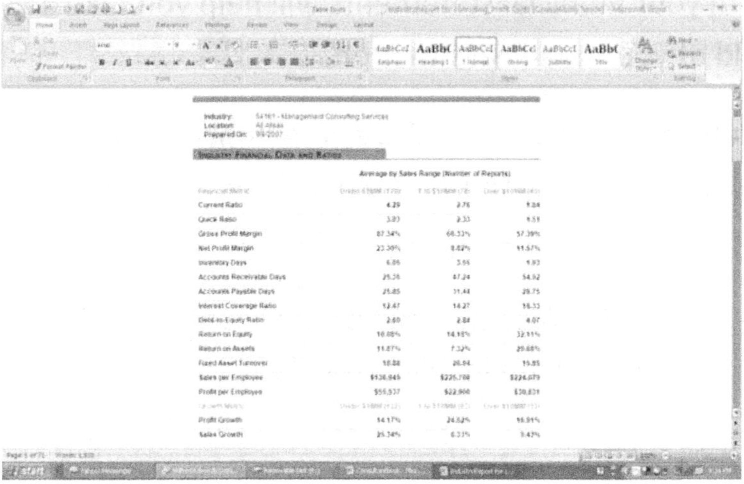

Industry: 54161 - Management Consulting Services
Location: All Areas
Prepared On: [illegible]-2007

INDUSTRY FINANCIAL DATA AND RATIOS

	Average by Sales Range (Number of Reports)		
Financial Metric	[illegible]	[illegible]	[illegible]
Current Ratio	4.29	2.76	7.84
Quick Ratio	3.83	2.33	4.51
Gross Profit Margin	87.34%	68.33%	57.39%
Net Profit Margin	23.30%	8.62%	11.57%
Inventory Days	6.86	3.66	4.93
Accounts Receivable Days	25.36	47.24	54.92
Accounts Payable Days	25.85	31.44	29.75
Interest Coverage Ratio	13.47	14.27	16.33
Debt-to-Equity Ratio	2.60	2.84	4.07
Return on Equity	10.88%	14.15%	32.11%
Return on Assets	11.87%	7.32%	29.88%
Fixed Asset Turnover	18.88	26.94	15.85
Sales per Employee	$136,945	$235,708	$224,679
Profit per Employee	$55,537	$22,900	$30,831
Growth Metric	[illegible]	[illegible]	[illegible]
Profit Growth	14.17%	24.52%	16.91%
Sales Growth	25.34%	6.33%	3.42%

Figure 7: Industry Ratios

Here is an idea of what the industry standard information is for consultants. Look at your financials and see how you compare. Use the table at the back of the book (page 104) to assist you with the calculations.

Using your Profit & Loss Statement and Balance Sheet will provide you with the financial data you need for the calculations. Again, this is where working with me, or your own professional management accountant, to calculate your ratios from your financial statements will help you take a hold of your financial situation.

What are some potential ways to improve the company's ability to meet obligations as they come due?

1. Monitor Accounts Receivable continuously. Follow up on invoices regularly to ensure the business is receiving payments in a timely fashion.

2. Avoid pre-paying expenses or Accounts Payable. The reason is to keep funds inside the business (potentially earning interest) for as long as possible. It is generally not a good idea to pay bills earlier than the terms agreed upon -- utilize trade credit fully. Discounts may be an exception.

3. Increase prices selectively where possible. Done effectively, this can boost cash flow and liquidity. Good Income Statement

management helps Balance Sheet performance.

4. Eliminate or reduce some overhead or fixed costs to reduce monthly expenses. Small decreases in overhead will typically yield large cash savings over time, especially if fixed costs can be reduced (those costs which tend to stay the same over time).

5. Sell things that can boost cash such as unproductive assets. These are assets that are not contributing sufficiently to the generation of income and cash flow (possibly because they are under-utilized).

6. Prepare yearly forecasts that show cash flow levels at various points in time. Consider updating these forecasts on a monthly or even bi-weekly basis. This can help predict/prepare for potential cash shortfalls that may occur in the future.

7. Bill customers more quickly in order to speed up the collection process (billing cycle) and get funds into the business faster. If customers are billed, on average, even three days earlier each month, the business's cash position can improve significantly.

8. Apply and collect late fees on delinquent Accounts Receivable when possible -- charge interest on past due invoices.

9. Try to establish a sufficient line of credit from the bank. There are methods to determine the amount of short-term credit needed to run the business. Talking with the bank can be helpful in this area. The business should obtain, but not necessarily use, as much financing as possible from the bank.

10. Monitor the impact tax payments may have on cash. Reserve adequate funds to allow you to meet future tax obligations based on earnings.

11. Monitor the amount of money that is being used for activities unrelated to the business. An example could be money taken out of the business on draws to principals.

What are some things the company might do to develop favorable profitability trends?

1. Monitor the profit generated per individual client and focus business on the most profitable. Determine what aspects make those clients more profitable and if other clients can be turned more profitable.

2. Monitor operating costs (labor charges) continuously, because it is easy for the company to get "bloated". In this industry, operating costs as a percentage of revenue should be about 30-35% of revenue.

3. Create good monthly budgets with cost reduction goals, broken down by account, that are put right into an accounting system (chart of accounts). This should allow

management the ability to pull "variance reports". These reports compare budgeted revenues and expenses with actual revenues and expenses and can help managers keep costs down.

4. Generate accurate financial reports on a timely basis -- within 15 days of the end of the financial period. This will help ensure the usefulness of the data for examination purposes. Good financial reports are the backbone of management decisions.

5. Monitor the costs going into all office supplies. With more important costs being monitored closely, many businesses forget to look at this smaller cost, and often allow it to be higher than necessary.

What are some things the company can consider to encourage sales growth?

1. Implement a solid job cost system, to recognize revenue properly. Revenues are

best recognized by using the percentage of completion methodology, based upon labor dollars.

2. Diversify your consulting revenue. It is easy to become dependent upon single client relationships or single lines of services. Larger, successful businesses are now offering more and different types of services than they did five years ago.

3. Provide clients with easy access to the business for follow up questions. This can help establish the business as one that cares about providing clients with quality service.

4. Develop a niche for specific industries. Use trade fairs and trade publications to market the business offering to potential clients.

5. Use client surveys. Send confidential surveys to clients and ask them how the business might better meet their needs.

The surveys should ask both specific and general questions about how to improve services. By getting information from clients, the business will be able to better meet needs, which will increase sales/revenue over time.

6. Have an attractive web presence. This will potentially increase revenue by providing an extra forum for the business to feature its offerings. Consider consulting a marketing/design firm to get tips for improvement.

7. Work to consistently meet the expectations of clients. Clarify client expectations up front, when necessary. Effectively meeting client expectations is often central to obtaining repeat business.

8. Work to establish clear and consistent identifiers so clients can quickly recognize the business. Each forum where the business features itself, whether it is in a

magazine or a website, should help clients quickly identify the business and its offerings.

9. Create a reputation as a quality provider in order to help generate referrals from clients. Word-of-mouth is often a free form of advertising for the business.

10. Make it known to clients that their business is appreciated. For example, thanking clients for their business after each interaction is often a simple act that can help make clients feel valued.

11. Display the achievements of the business where appropriate. For example, obtain and display testimonials and/or awards won. This can help establish the business as a quality provider to potential clients.

12. Work on getting free publicity when possible. An example could be contributing to a newspaper or magazine article on a

subject associated with the business. Often, being a part of articles can build credibility among clients. In addition, this can help build name recognition, which can potentially attract additional clients.

Knowing your financial position is the key to success. Now the challenge is upon you to make it happen. Contact your accounting professional and make it happen sooner than later. Best of luck and let me know how I can help you – pam@rppc.net.

DON'T FORGET

1.

2.

3.

CALCULATE YOUR RATIOS

NOW WHAT?

The first and foremost part of having a good consulting business is the personal aspects you will bring to the business. What is your area of expertise? You most likely spend hours each year honing your skills through continuing education, reading, and various other activities. The key is that your business process needs attention to it as well and that is what this book should have provided to you. It is full of tips that you need to implement in the day-to-day operations of your business and how you run it.

You must implement the areas we have just covered to ensure that you have a profitable consulting business. That should be your overall goal. Enjoy what you are doing and make money too! Find yourself a good management accountant who can help you in any of these areas listed in this book. With time you will feel comfortable with the concepts but hire a professional to make the process simpler. You now know what areas you need to address – use this book and any other available resource to make it happen. If you need my help, don't hesitate to ask (www.rppc.net).

PAM'S RESOURCES

Boost Your Bottom Line – www.consultantsboostyourbottomline.com

Out of the Red – www.getoutofthered.com

Articles – www.pamnewmanarticles.com

Speaking – www.pamnewmanspeaker.com

Consulting – www.rppc.net (Realizing Profitable Potential through Change)

Pam provides a full range of services including one-on-one consulting in person and via phone in addition to speaking and writing for various groups and organizations.

RATIO CALCULATIONS

RATIO	*CALCULATION*	*WHAT DOES IT TELL YOU?*
CURRENT RATIO	CURRENT ASSETS/ CURRENT LIABILITIES	SHORT-TERM DEBT-PAYING ABILITY
ACID-TEST RATIO	(CASH + SHORT TERM INVESTMENTS + CURRENT RECEIVABLES)/ CURRENT LIABILITIES	IMMEDIATE SHORT-TERM DEBT-PAYING ABILITY
ACCOUNTS RECEIVABLE TURNOVER	NET SALES/ AVERAGE ACCOUNTS RECEIVABLE	EFFICIENCY OF COLLECTIONS
TOTAL ASSET TURNOVER	NET SALES/ AVERAGE TOTAL ASSETS	EFFICIENCY OF ASSETS IN PRODUCING SALES
DEBT RATIO	TOTAL LIABILITIES/ TOTAL ASSETS	CREDITOR FINANCING
EQUITY RATIO	TOTAL EQUITY/ TOTAL ASSETS	OWNER FINANCING
PROFIT MARGIN RATIO	NET INCOME/ NET SALES	NET INCOME IN EACH SALES DOLLAR
GROSS MARGIN RATIO	(NET SALES – COST OF GOODS SOLD)/ NET SALES	GROSS MARGIN IN EACH SALES DOLLAR
RETURN ON TOTAL ASSETS	NET INCOME/ AVERAGE TOTAL ASSETS OR PROFIT MARGIN RATIO * TOTAL ASSET TURNOVER	OVERALL PROFITABILITY OF ASSETS
CONTRIBUTION MARGIN RATIO	(NET SALES – VARIABLE COSTS)/ NET SALES	PORTION OF SELLING PRICE THAT EXCEEDS VARIABLE COSTS
BREAK-EVEN POINT IN DOLLARS	FIXED COSTS/ CONTRIBUTION MARGIN RATIO	TOTAL EXPENSES=TOTAL INCOME

ORDER FORM

Fax Order to: RPPC, Inc. 816.256.5487

Call for Quantity discounts over 20.

Boost Your Bottom Line	____ @ 12.95	
Out of the Red	____ @ 12.95	
Sets (1 of each)	____ @ 19.95	
Shipping/Handling		5.95
Total	$ ____________	

Shipping/Billing:

Name:

Address:

City/State/Zip:

Visa/MC #:

Expiration Date:

Signature:

ABOUT THE AUTHOR

Pam Newman, President of RPPC, Inc. has a diverse background with extensive experience in businesses ranging from entrepreneurial start-ups to Fortune 500 organizations. Industries include academic, banking, construction, consulting, restaurant, telecommunications, and more. Pam's passion is helping entrepreneurs in realizing profitable potential by changing the way they run their business. Pam is also the author of ***Out of the Red*** and writes articles for various publications including www.entrepreneur.com.

Pam divides her time between individual consulting, group trainings and speaking engagements. If you would be interested in having her speak to your organization, contact us toll free at 1.866.206.0824.

Made in the USA
Monee, IL
04 November 2026

67380509R00066